CLEVER RIDDLES AND JOKES

FOR

SMART KIDS

GAINING KNOWLEDGE WHILE HAVING FUN

O. J MARVIN

DEDICATION

Firstly this work is dedicated to God almighty for His unconditional love for me and to every depressed person out there.

TABLE OF CONTENT

CHAPTER ONE:

CHAPTER TWO:

CHAPTER THREE:

CHAPTER FOUR:

CHAPTER FIVE:

CHAPTER SIX:

CHAPTER SEVEN:

CHAPTER 1

FUNS OF RIDDLES

Aside from taking vanilla ice cream, nothing interests or excites kids like riddles. Riddles aren't only fun; they are mind booster and are a sure way of improving children's verbal fluency and creative thinking. Riddles often erupt from things we take common or that have deep undertones and meanings. Apart from the fun and laughter that accompanies riddles, riddles pass serious messages and wisdom that could help children develop a logical and critical thinking mind. For you to effectively solve riddles, always bear in mind that riddles could be presented in such a way that it distracts your attention from the actual answer, even when it's right there in front of you. Sometimes a hint would be given but deeply sandwiched or disguised in distracting words, so look beyond the literary meaning and deduce the riddles' answer. Usually, riddles are crafted or coined in a puzzling or misleading way. Many have a double or hidden meaning.

Some riddles could be a funny comment whose answer is as simple as ABC. In contrast, others could be very hard and importune you to crack your brain before you can deduce the meaning or answer.

In the past, riddles are part of the responsibilities every caring parent owes their children; this is because riddles have several moral undertones aside from the fun and laughter it brings. Modern society and its parenting style hardly have time for their children because of the demands of their jobs and other economic commitments, making riddle cracking a fast eroding culture.

History of Riddles

Riddles have strong nexus to old English poetry. The etiological proof of riddles is found in the work of Plato and Aristotle. Riddles were used as an artifice to display wit and sagacity in ancient Greece.

Poets used riddles to express themselves. When a poem embodies some riddle elements, it fascinates the reader's mind, and the writer can successfully get their message across in a more interesting way.

If you want to use a single stone to kill two birds, then riddles are the best stone to use; this is because kids of all ages love solving riddles;

while solving this riddle and having fun, learning is also taking place. Riddle is a no dulling and fascinating way of engaging children to pick interest in learning, particularly boring subjects because of its fun-filled attributes. Riddles have several learning and developmental benefits, and below are some of the benefits.

Benefits of Riddles

Riddles benefits kids in the following ways:

It helps develop a sense of humor. As you pick interest in riddles, over time, you will realize yourself trying to come up with some funny and ridiculous comments that make people laugh; and as you develop yourself, as time goes on, you will be perceived as having a sense of humor. This helps you to see and embrace things in a more positive light and help eliminate boredom.

Stimulate interest in reading comprehension. Nothing is as funny and fulfilling as watching kids attempt telling and solving riddles. They love it because it is a learning process filled with fun and excitement, and as they indulge themselves, they develop more love for reading and learning.

It helps children to pay undivided attention to details. Riddles help children develop good listening skills, thus making them grasp important details. The knowledge they acquire from riddles is shared with siblings, friends, teachers, and even parents, therefore inculcating socialization in children.

Creates Bonds. Riddles give you the chance to establish a strong bond between you and your children and help children develop a strong bond between them and their peers, which sometimes helps them break the hold of shyness and gives kids some sense of accomplishment.

Help children to develop problem-solving and critical thinking mind. Teaches Problem-solving skills. Since problems are an integral part of human society, tackling and solving them becomes vital; riddles help equip kids with these skills.

Enhance or boost language skills and linguistic awareness. As kids read and solve riddles, they are constantly getting acquainted with the new and interesting words, thereby expanding their vocabulary. They learn new words and their meanings and ways to use them metaphorically and in a different context.

Promote critical and analytical thinking and deductive reasoning. Critical thinking is a vital skill kids need to have and explore to solve riddles. As kids solve riddles, they learn how to think more in-depth, which critically improves comprehension and creativity.

CHAPTER 2

EASY RIDDLES

Here are some hilarious riddles for smart kids, teens, adults, and the whole family; to help you strengthen the family bond and to take this Christmas celebration to a different dimension of ecstasy. These riddles and jokes guarantee to make this Christmas a memorable one. It is packed with several moral lessons riddles that will undoubtedly transform the mind of kids to imbibe honesty and Godliness and engraving indelibly in their hearts that the fear of the Lord is the beginning of all Wisdom.

The riddles and jokes come in a different format, ranging from easy to hard; animal riddles, Math riddles, nation riddles, moral and general riddles, and lots more. They are crafted in a way never before seen; some, you may be familiar with, others may be new to you, which makes the whole process funny and exciting.

Every category of riddles has their answers directly on the next page, with some answers presented in detail to make you understand the riddles even more.

EASY RIDDLES

1. I am something, I am part and parcel of a whole, but when I am placed back inside

the whole, I find myself losing form. What am I?

2. I am something; I can never be locked up or concealed in a building. What am I?

3. I am something, I amend torn clothes, yet I cannot amend myself, what am I?

4. I am something people use everywhere; I have so many branches, yet no fruits, leaves, or trunk. What am I?

5. What is that thing that leaves you when in darkness?

6. I am something, the more of me that you see, the less you see, what am I?

7. What is that thing that when you cut for use, makes you shed tears?

8. I am something; my existence depends on the presence of another element. What am I?

9. I am something; no one has ever seen me with the naked eyes, neither do they know where I come from nor where I am heading, yet they feel my presence when I pass. What am I?

10. What is that thing that is black when clean and white when dirty?

11. What is that thing that gets bigger when you take more of it outside?

12. What is that thing that is so light, yet the world's strongest man can't hold for three minutes

13. I am something, in my world, today come before yesterday, what am I?

14. I am something, I have something that is exclusively mine, yet others use it more than I do. What am I?

15. I am something; you can only catch me but can't throw me. What am I?

16. I am something, I have so many words inside of me to relate, yet I never speak. What am I?

17. I am something, I taste better than I smell, what am I?

18. I am something, you will always see me where construction is going on when you remove the first two letters from my name, and I become one. What am I?

19. I am something; I always occupy rooms without taking up any space. What am I?

20. I am something; I always give people an exact copy of themselves when they appear before me. What am I?

21. I am something, I always break without falling and fall without breaking, what am I?

22. What is that thing that is always in front of every human being, yet cannot be seen?

23. I am something, I prevent people from getting wet, yet I can't prevent myself from getting wet. What am I?

24. I am something, I travel every day, and my destination is always west, what am I?

25. What is the name of the longest iron snake on Earth that do not move on grass?

26. I am something, I never ask questions, yet often answered, what am I?

27. What is that thing that dies even though it is not a living thing?

28. Eyelogologosisiasis who can spell that?

ANSWERS TO EASY RIDDLES

1. ANSWER: Ice; when it is returned into the water, it melts.

2. ANSWER: Smoke

3. ANSWER: A Needle

4. ANSWER: A Bank

5. ANSWER: Your Shadow

6. ANSWER: Darkness

7. ANSWER: Onion

8. ANSWER: Smoke; you have to start a fire before you can see smoke

9. ANSWER: Air/ Cool Breeze

10. ANSWER: A chalkboard

11. ANSWER: A Hole

12. ANSWER: Breath

13. ANSWER: Dictionary

14. ANSWER: Your Name

15. ANSWER: Cold

16. ANSWER: A Book

17. ANSWER: Tongue

18. ANSWER: Stone; when you remove the first two letters "ST" you get one

19. ANSWER: Light

20. ANSWER: Mirror

21. ANSWER: Day and Night

22. ANSWER: The Future

23. ANSWER: Umbrella

24. ANSWER: Sun; it rises from the East and sets in the West

25. ANSWER: A Train

26. ANSWER: A Door Bell

27. ANSWER: Battery

28. ANSWER: T-H-A-T> THAT

CHAPTER 3

HARD RIDDLES

1. What are those things that no matter how much they quarrel with each other, nothing can stop them from cooperating and living together?

2. My enemy's name and I start with the letter F, yet no matter how you try to make peace between us by pairing us together, we get aggravated or provoked the more, what are we?

3. What is that thing that you most have to dig the Earth and make proper

arrangement for before it survival can be guaranteed?

4. What is the name of the place that, irrespective of where you are in the world, your takeoff time, or age, you all must arrive at the same destination?

5. I look like a bulb, I am single from the outside, yet I have many siblings; each of my siblings dutifully wraps up its immediate younger sibling. What am I?

6. We are two important things found in people's homes, but we become one thing people often step on in the sitting room whenever we are brought together or combined. What are we?

7. I am something, I am a very loyal friend of humans, my favorite spot is in the kitchen, but when I am left carelessly or

uncontrolled I could cause serious havoc, what am I?

8. I am something, I go into hiding during the day, but at night I am found scintillating everywhere, what am I?

9. What is that thing that is everywhere during the day but can never be found at night, no matter how you search for it?

10. I am something I contain seven letters. My name's entire meaning signifies a great woman, yet the first two and first four letters of my name have a male undertone. What am I?

11. I am something, people who create me don't need me, people who buy me don't use me, and the person who eventually uses me do not see, feel, or know that it's using me. What am I?

12. I am something, you can find in me lakes without water, a forest without trees, mountains without stones, cities without people, what am I?

13. What is that thing that doesn't run after animals before catching them?

14. Last weekend, I was in a club with so many people dancing with each other, as the music was about getting interesting, I noticed that nobody left the dance hall yet no single person was dancing. How is that possible?

15. After a plane crash one Saturday morning, every single passenger on board lost their lives; who then survived?

16. I am something, in my world, I am so liberal that I allow success to come before work. What am I?

17.I am something; I only trade or transact business with blood money. What am I?

18.What is that thing that only visits female who is of age monthly?

19.What kind of top can you carry on your laps?

20.I am something; you just have to hit me on the head to drive me through the woods. What am I?

21.What is that profession that when you remove the last three letters from its name and split the remaining into two halves would leave you with a car and pen to behold?

22.What rank of the military force is said to war and rant a lot?

23.What is that thing that no matter how powerful you are, you can't afford to be enemy?

24. What is that thing that goes up whenever it rains?

25. I am something, I have been in existence from the beginning of creation, yet each time I come out, I appear young, grow up, and disappear and come back again. What am I?

26. I am one of the parts found on the human head; no matter how the eyes turn around to look at me, they can't. What am I?

27. What bet can't be won, regardless of how sure the odds are?

28. I am something; I often compel tall people to bend their heads. What am I?

29. He has wedded many women but has never been married. Who is he?

30. What is the leader's name that no matter how you follow him, never follow you home?

31. I am something, you find me suspended everywhere in the world, yet not a singular pillar is seen holding or supporting me; what am I?

32. What does a talebearer do?

33. I am a word, I contain just five letters, and I happen to be the longest word in the dictionary because of the word I form when my first letter is removed. What am I?

34. I am something, I make people get back on their feet when they fall sick, but when the first letter of my name is removed, the same people place me beneath their center table. What am I?

35. What drum doesn't make a sound, instead it is damage by loud and violent sound?

36. What craft allows you to fly even when you are not a pilot?

37. What type of ship carry and allow students to sail through in quest of knowledge without collecting a single penny from them?

38. What type of phone makes only sounds, but you cannot call or be called, or even make use of data or air time?

39. What sea make pirates fall sick and even vomit whenever they sail across in their ships

40. Forward, I am a cold dish of vegetables, but when the first two letters of my name are removed, I become a boy. What am I?

ANSWERS TO HARD RIDDLES

1. ANSWER: Teeth and Tongue; teeth sometimes bite the tongue, yet they remain in the mouth.

2. ANSWER: Fire and Fuel

3. ANSWER: Building; you must first dig a foundation and have the bricks well

    laid before proper building can commence.

4. ANSWER: Grave; regardless of where you are, your age, and when you die, you must always end in the grave.

5. ANSWER: Onion

6. ANSWER: Car + Pet = Carpet

7. ANSWER: Fire

8. ANSWER: The Stars

9. ANSWER: Sun

10. ANSWER: Heroine; the first two letters "HE" for male and the first four letters "HERO" also for male.

11. ANSWER: A Casket; the person that creates it doesn't need it, the person that buys it doesn't use it, and the person that uses it, don't even see or know it's using it.

12. ANSWER: A Map

13. ANSWER: Trap

14. ANSWERS: All the Dancers are couples

15. ANSWER: All the couples

16. ANSWER: Dictionary

17. ANSWER: Vampires

18. ANSWER: Menstrual cycle

19.ANSWER: Laptop

20.ANSWER: A nail; which must be hit on the head before it can enter the wood

21.ANSWER: Carpenter; when you remove the last three letters, you get Carpen, and when you split into two, you get Car and Pen

22.ANSWER: Warrant officers

23.ANSWER: Water

24.ANSWER: Umbrella

25.ANSWER: The Moon

26.ANSWER: The Ears

27.ANSWER: Alphabet

28.ANSWER: A Door Frame; whenever you hit your head on a door frame, you learn to bend so as not to hit your head again.

29. ANSWER: A Roman Catholic Priest who weds a couple in the church but can't get married.

30. ANSWER: The road, the road may direct you everywhere, and even down to your house, but will never follow you home

31. ANSWER: Sky

32. ANSWER: Reveal secrets

33. ANSWER: Smile; when you remove the first letter "s" you get a mile

34. ANSWER: Drug; when the first letter is removed, it becomes rug.

35. ANSWER: Ear Drum

36. ANSWER: Witchcraft

37. ANSWER: Scholarship

38. ANSWER: Saxophone.

39. ANSWER: Nausea.

40. ANSWER: Salad, when you remove the first two letters, you have lad left, and lad simply means a boy.

CHAPTER 4

ANIMAL RIDDLES

1. What is that thing, that no matter how hard you try to clean it up, will always return to the dirt?

2. I am a loyal friend and ally to humans but an enemy to my kind. What am I?

3. What is that thing that assumes any color in any environment it finds itself in?

4. I am something, no matter how high you throw me up, I never land on my back, what am I?

5. I am something, I bear the name of two different animals, what am I?

6. We are three animals with keys, yet we can't open any door, what are we?

7. What is that thing that announces the break of dawn yet never grows teeth?

8. What is that thing that doesn't have money, wealth or influence, but always seen in the palace of kings?

9. What is that creature that is small, smart, hardworking, and provides its food in the summer?

10. What creatures have no king, yet all of them march in rank?

11. What creatures are small yet make their homes in the rocks?

12. I am something, I am the worst singer on planet earth, yet whenever I sing, people must clap for me. What am I?

13. What is that thing that elephants never pray for?

14. Why is it that the food of frogs is never found on a tree?

15. Why is it that crickets often make their holes by the footpath?

16. We are two things: one is often spread on bread, and the other is not good to perch on food, but we form a beautiful and colorful insect when combined. What are we?

17. Why do termites have a big head and strong mandibles?

18. What is that animal whose head looks like a mouse and hangs upside down during the day in a dark shade?

19. Why does the owl have a big head and round bulge eyes?

20. Why is the vulture bald and said to be a patient bird?

21. What is that animal that hides her young in her front pocket?

22. What animal parades itself as though in a fashion parade and elegantly displays its feathers?

23. Why is the Hen and Duck not friends?

24. If kangaroos were athletes, what sport would they be great at?

25. Forward I am a small bird, but when the first two letters of my name are removed, I become something that kills. What am I?

26. What is that creature that carries a load bigger than itself on the back moves slowly because of the load's weight?

27.I am a king with no crown and no subject to rule. My favorite covering is blue, and I dive into the water to catch fish. What am I?

28.Forward, I am a soft-bodied creature with a shell, but the moment the first letter of my name gives way, I become something found mostly in the hands of carpenters. What am I?

ANSWERS TO ANIMAL RIDDLES

1. ANSWER: Pigs.

2. ANSWER: Dogs; are close to humans and are used for hunting other wild animals.

3. ANSWER: Chameleon

4. ANSWER: A Cat

5. ANSWER: Cat + Fish= Catfish

6. ANSWER: Monkey, Donkey, and Turkey

7. ANSWER: A cockerel/Rooster

8. ANSWER: Lizards

9. ANSWER: Ants

10. ANSWER: Locusts

11. ANSWER: Badgers

12.ANSWER: Mosquito

13.ANSWER: To be big

14.ANSWER: Because Frogs cannot climb

15.ANSWER: They are praise seekers

16.ANSWER: Butter and fly; when combine, you get Butterfly

17.ANSWER: Because of their arduous task of eating woods.

18.ANSWER: Bat

19.ANSWER: To see and learn the secrets of the night

20.ANSWER: Because the wisdom in its head is too much for hair to grow on it

21.ANSWER: Kangaroo

22.ANSWER: Peacock

23.ANSWER: Because the Hen doesn't bath as the Duck do

24.ANSWER: long jump

25. ANSWER: Sparrow; when you remove the first two letters, it becomes an arrow. Arrows kill

26. ANSWER: Snail; its shell is always bigger than its body, and it moves slowly.

27. ANSWER: Kingfisher

28. ANSWER: Snail; remove 'S,' and you have a nail.

CHAPTER 5

MATH RIDDLES

1. I am something, I contain just six letters, but when you remove the last letter from me, I automatically become twelve (12). What am I?

2. What city can be deduced from the United States of America when 3/7 chicken, 2/3 cat, and 2/4 goat are deducted, respectively.

3. How many seconds are there from January to June?

4. What words are deduced when 4/6 golden, 3/10 medication, and 2/5 allow are deducted, respectively

ANSWERS TO MATHS RIDDLES

1. ANSWER: Dozens, when you remove the letter "S" you get dozen, and dozen implies twelve (12)

2. ANSWER: Chicago.

3. ANSWER: Six seconds; 2nd of January, 2nd of February, 2nd of March, 2nd of April, 2nd of May, and 2nd of June.

4. ANSWER: Gold Medal

CHAPTER 6

NATION RIDDLES

1. What nation in the world is reputed for her lawless and horrific acts?

2. What city in the world is reputed for shocking?

3. What country in the world is famous for her appetite?

4. What nation of the world is famous for the act of postponing, delaying, or putting off her responsibility to her citizens, especially out of habitual

carelessness or laziness on the path of her citizens and government?

5. What nation in the world is famous for her brightness due to her power generating capacity?

6. I am found in Europe, and when the first and last letters of my name are removed, I become a State in an African Country Nigeria, what am I?

7. I am a country in Europe, I contain just six letters, but when the letters of my name are divided into two halves, the first part becomes Can and the second a name generally identified with firstborn daughters in Igbo tradition in Nigeria. What am I?

8. What is the name of the nation famous for her intellectual dexterity, especially

in testing her citizens' knowledge or intelligence quotient (IQ) regularly?

9. What city is the most liberal city on Earth?

10. What nation of the world is the most criticized for her evil practices and corruption?

11. What land is famous for cold?

12. What nation of the world has fake, false, counterfeit, and unrealistic government and citizens in the world?

13. What nation in the middle-east is chosen and consecrated by God?

14. What powerful nation of the world is formed due to the conflation of several distinct states?

15. What nation of the world do you have to die and come back in another body

before you can be confirmed as a bona fide citizen?

ANSWERS TO NATION RIDDLES

1. ANSWER: Abomination

2. ANSWER: Electricity

3. ANSWER: Hungary

4. ANSWER: Procrastination; this implies delay, postponement, or complete avoidance, the part where a nation is mentioned is just to distract you from the needful.

5. ANSWER: Illumination

6. ANSWER: London; when you remove the first and last letters, you get Ondo. One of the States in the western region of Nigeria

7. ANSWER: Canada; when split gives you Can and Ada

8. ANSWER: Examination

9. ANSWER: Generosity

10.ANSWER: Condemnation

11.ANSWER: Iceland

12.ANSWER: Imagination

13.ANSWER: ordination

14.ANSWER: Combination

15.ANSWER: Reincarnation

CHAPTER 7

MORAL AND GENERAL RIDDLES

1. What must you fear to increase in knowledge and wisdom?

2. I am something; no matter how long I am concealed or denied, I will always prevail. What am I?

3. What is that thing that pays attention, listens, and hears even more than the ears?

4. What is the name of that part of the body that takes all the glory when other parts perform their functions?

5. What is that thing that often steals people's time but never makes use of it?

6. I am something; when clay and butter are placed under me, my effect makes one hard and melts the other. What am I?

7. What is that thing that is so sweet when tasted, but you have to endure some stings to get it?

8. I am something; I am the driver of every beautiful and positive human invention. What am I?

9. I am something; no matter how tall I grow, I still bend in obedience to my owner. What am I?

10. I am something, I am very difficult to make or gather simultaneously, I am very easy to get rid of, what am I?

11. What is that institution that gives you a certificate even before your first-semester exam?

12. What is that debt that everyone owes, regardless of how rich they are?

13. I am something, to be a good top, I must be a loyal and good bottom, what am I?

14. I am something nobody wants to relate with me, yet I am an undeniable part of society's reality. What am I?

15. What are those things that will never accompany you to your final home no matter how you accumulate them?

16. What is that thing that easily forgets all the good accorded it the moment it's angry?

17. I am something, the government of every nation fight and kick against me, yet I am part and parcel of every government system, what am I?

18. I am a being no one had seen, I applaud and encourage you when you do the wrong things and take you as an enemy when you do the right thing, what am I?

19. The word impossible does not exist in my world; what am I?

20. Uncreated yet made all things; what am I?

21. What is that thing you see whenever you see pride?

22. What is that thing that always accompanies humility?

23. What is that thing that is not weighed on the scale yet outweighs the weight of sand and stone put together?

24. What are those three things that are never satisfied, and the fourth one never say enough?

25. What is that one thing that is sharper than the knife?

26. What is said to be the crown of every husband?

27. What is that thing that gossips never do?

28. What type of tooth doesn't grasp, tear, chew, or grind meat?

29. Why is the female toad always seen backing the male?

30. What is that cream that doesn't lighten up or moisturizes your skin but is cold when used?

31. What social media will join and become a star that weighs only in grams and not kilograms?

32. What book allows you to read and write without opening a single page?

33. I am a country that loves soccer, but when the first letter of my name is removed, I become a pain that nobody loves. What am I?

34. I belong to a club where everybody is sane, but when you remove the last three letters of my name, I become really mad. What am I?

35. A person who loves liver and swims in a swimming pool often should be given a free ticket to watch which club in Europe as a reward for being a super fan?

36. Football is what we play, yet our name speaks of weapons of war; what are we?

37. What is the name of the sea that allows only blue ships loaded with footballers to float?

38. Football is what we play, yet the beginning of our name suggests we are sprinters, and when the last three letters of our name are removed, we become mad. What are we?

ANSWERS TO MORAL AND GENERAL RIDDLES

1. ANSWER: The fear of the lord

2. ANSWER: Truth; no matter the situation, truth always prevails.

3. ANSWER: Our Body (skin); when the body is beaten or subjected to some pain, it compels you to be more obedient because you wouldn't want to experience pain the second time.

4. ANSWER: The mouth; for instance, when the legs walk, the mouth would say I walk a long distance today when the eyes see, the mouth will

announce what it saw when the ears hear, the mouth would say what I heard today was good or bad, or when your stomach is filled up to the point of discomfort, the mouth would say I ate too much thus always claiming their glory by announcing what they did.

5. ANSWER: Procrastination

6. ANSWER: Sun; this could also be likened to a saying that people have different destinies. What didn't favor you may favor another, so never stop trying. A place that is a curse for someone may turn out to be a blessing for others.

7. ANSWER: Honey, this also implies "Success", success is very sweet when attained or achieved, but it

doesn't come easily; it entails hard work and perspiration.

8. ANSWER: Idea; every invention came from a tiny idea rooted in the mind of the inventor.

9. ANSWER: Okra plant, no matter the height of Okra plant, the owner still bends it during harvest; this implies that no matter how big, rich, influential a child gets, they still accord respect to their parents.

10. ANSWER: Money; very difficult to make but easy to spend

11. ANSWER: Marriage Institution

12. ANSWER: Death; we must all die someday

13. ANSWER: Leader and Follower; for you to be a good leader; you must be a good follower

14. ANSWER: Poverty

15. ANSWER: Riches and Wealth, no matter how you accumulate them, you will never be buried with any.

16. ANSWER: The Stomach, whenever it is hungry, doesn't remember how well it had been fed in the past; it just disturbs until its desires are met.

17. ANSWER: Corruption

18. ANSWER: The devil

19. ANSWER: God Almighty

20. ANSWER: God Almighty

21. ANSWER: Disgrace

22. ANSWER: Upliftment

23. ANSWER: A Fool's provocation

24. ANSWER: Hell, the barren womb, the Earth ever thirsty for water, and fire, which never says enough.

25. ANSWER: A loose tongue

26. ANSWER: A good Wife; she is a virtuous woman and brings honor to her husband, but she who brings shame is like rottenness in his bones

27. ANSWER: Talk about themselves

28. ANSWER: Blue tooth

29. ANSWER: Because she wouldn't want to lose him to another babe

30. ANSWER: Ice-cream

31. ANSWER: Instagram

32. ANSWER: Facebook

33. ANSWER: Spain; when you remove "s", you get pain

34. ANSWER: Real Madrid; when you remove the last three letters, you get real mad

35. ANSWER: Liverpool

36. ANSWER: Arsenal

37. ANSWER: Chelsea

38.ANSWER: Athletico Madrid

CHAPTER 8

JOKES

Below are some lovely and exciting jokes to make your Christmas a memorable one.

JOKE

A judge once asked a plaintiff in a court; what the bone of contention was? The plaintiff looked at the judge sternly in the eyes and replied! Is that what you are told? There is no bone of contention; there is only meat of contention between my greedy friend and me; just order him to give me my fair share of Christmas beef.

A class teacher once walked her student home and met his father, Mr. Shawn, at home.

Mr. Shawn: Hello, Miss Grace!

Miss Grace: Hi Mr. Shawn

Mr. Shawn: How is my son's performance this term?

Miss Grace: Not encouraging at all; your son finds it difficult to understand the simple addition of numbers.

Mr. Shawn: that is not possible, my son is very good at addition.

Miss Grace: Call your son and confirm things for yourself.

Mr. Shawn: Tony, is it true you don't understand the addition of numbers?

Tony was silent and was instead using his right foot to draw an imaginary line on the floor.

Mr. Shawn: Tony, tell me, two packs of spaghetti plus four packs of spaghetti will give you how many packs all together?

Tony: Six-packs sir

Mr. Shawn: Ten packs of noodles plus three packs of noodles will give you how many packs all together?

Tony: thirteen packs, sir.

Mr. Shawn: Four crates of eggs plus five crates of eggs will give you how many crates all together?

Tony: Nine crates of eggs, sir.

Miss Grace: wow, this is incredible; how are you able to do this?

Mr. Shawn: your teaching method is different from what my son is used to. You know my son is a glutton. You can tell from the weight that he eats a lot. When next you treat the addition of numbers with him, just make sure you use all the names of delicious meals you know. He will understand better.

JOKE

A father was angry at his son after seeing his report card for coming last in the class. He asked his son, why are you so dull? Why can't you be as brilliant as your friend and mate Jack? Nobody in my family is as dull as you are. When I was your age, I come first in every subject and at all times in class. Why can't you just emulate my footsteps?

The son was hurt and sprinted to his room. The next day, the boy sat his father down and asked him the following questions

Son: Dad, how old are you?

Father: I'm in my mid-fifties

Son: Are you older than Mark Zuckerberge?

Father: Yes, son

Son: What about Bill Gate and Jeff Bezos?

Father: we are probably age mates.

Son: why can't you be brilliant and be as rich as they are? Why are you as poor as a church rat? Mark, Bill, and Bezos are your mates, and they are billionaires while you are poor.

The moral of this joke; never to compare people; we are all different and with different destinies.

Engr. Jack is an American civil engineer; he visited an African country for the first time to train a team of engineers. Mr. Jack, in a conversation with Jacob, the spoke person of the African engineers, asked how long it takes to build a twenty-story building.

Jacob: two to three years.

Engr. Jack: in America, it takes two weeks

Engr. Jack saw a very tall building and asked Jacob; how long did it take to build that?

Jacob: ten to twelve years

Engr. Jack: in America, it takes two months

Engr. Jack saw yet another beautiful overhead bridge on their way back home and asked Jacob how long it took to construct the bridge. Jacob already knew what Engr. Jack was up to clear his throat and replied; this bridge was not here a while ago; it just appeared, the fastest ever constructed bridge. This reply sent a strong message to Engr. Jack and shutting him up because he now realized that Jacob knew he had been lying to him.

JOKE

A very rich millionaire who had no wife nor kids and was very lonely, his only friend and companion was a dog called diamond. Unfortunately, diamond died, and this dealt a devastating blow to the millionaire. The millionaire wept bitterly over his dog's death and decided to give the dog a befitting burial. The millionaire went to a nearby church to solicit the pastor's help and ask him to pray for his dog before laying the dog to rest.

Millionaire: Pastor, my dog just died

Pastor: Hard luck, brother

Millionaire: could you please come and say a word of prayer for my dog

Pastor: I am sorry I can't do that

Millionaire: why?

Pastor: is not right; it's just a pet

The millionaire, in disappointment, said I was hoping to get you to pray for the soul of my diamond- I already made plans to pay you and your choir the sum of $10 million so that my diamond could rest in peace; well, I will find another pastor who will. The millionaire moved to leave when he heard," why didn't you tell me that your dog was a born again Christian? Of course, I will come and pray for your diamond.

A man was found on London Bridge, repeatedly shouting 722, 722, 722……

Suddenly a patrolling police officer came by and asked him, Mr., are you ok?

The man was still shouting 722, 722, 722……, so the police officer moved closer to him to find out what was amiss with the man. The man just held the officer by the neck and threw him over the Bridge and started shouting 723,723, 723………

Immediately all the passers-by and people around took to their heels after realizing the meaning of his count.

A man was known for how ugly he looks; as a matter of fact, he was the world's undisputed record holder of the ugliest man alive. He held this record for years and got tired because he thought that someday someone uglier would emerge and break his record, but none was forthcoming, so he got really tired and fed up and committed suicide. Immediately his soul left his body and headed for the land of the dead, on arrival; he was told to go to heaven since he suffered humiliation while alive, that he was going to find solace there. The man immediately walked toward heaven, and when he finally got to the gate, he knocks, and the Angel on duty open the gate and asked him to go away, that heaven doesn't harbor the souls of people that committed suicide; that he should go to hell at once. The man immediately found himself at the gate of hell and knocked. The demon on duty opened the gate saw the man immediately; the demon took to his heels and was shouting master, master on the top of his voice. The demon's master was, of course, sleeping when the distress shout of one of his demons woke him up. The devil had not completely regained consciousness from sleep when he opened his eyes faintly and saw the man coming from afar, the devil; out of fear shouted blood of Jesus, the blood of Jesus, and asked the demon what the man was doing in his kingdom, immediately the devil ran away shouting go and form your kingdom, this place is too small for us.

JOKE

A travel guide asked a Kenya boy who doesn't understand much of the English language on his first tourist trip to America. How do you do?

The Kenyan boy replied, 'I do as Audu do

Jack: Shawn, what other bonds do we have aside from covalent bond and electrovalent bond?

Shawn: We have Vagabond

Jack: can you believe what happen last weekend at my residence?

Shawn: what happened?

Jack: Armed robbers came to my house and stole my swimming pool

Jack: do you know what Africans do to bird flu?

Shawn: no

Jack: they eat the bird and bury the flu, so you see covid-19 won't thrive there.

Jack had been crushing on Sharon for a long time. One bright Saturday morning, Jack summoned the courage and approached Sharon for the very first time. Their conversation when thus:

Jack: Sharon, who owns the ATM to your POS?

Sharon: I don't understand

Jack: I mean, who controls the key to your sweet padlock?

Sharon: I still don't understand

Jack: Why are you behaving like a baby? I mean, do you have a boyfriend?

Sharon: I have an army of boyfriends. Would you like to join the queue?

Jack: I wouldn't mind, but I want to join as a general and not as a recruit.

Jack: Shawn, what is the opposite of fantastic

Shawn: the opposite of fantastic is cocastic

Jack: Shawn, what is the opposite of nonplus

Shawn: Nonminus

Jack: Why does Santa Clause have white beards?

Shawn: A sign of experience in charity works

Jack: What is the opposite of Minimum?

Shawn: MiniDad

Jack: What is the opposite of menopause?

Shawn: Menomove

Jack: What is the opposite of Adam's apple?

Shawn: Eve's Apple

Jack: What is the opposite of kidnap?

Shawn: Adult nap

Jack: What is the opposite of understand?

Shawn: Under sit

Jack: What is the opposite of matriculate?

Shawn: Matricu-early

Jack: what is the opposite of committee?

Shawn: commi-milk

MORAL QUOTES

❖ A child who bullies his or her mate lack sense, but he who remains silent has understanding.

❖ A child who is open to reproves turns out to be wise, but he who hates reproves soon turns out to be a scoffer.

- Little children, stolen water is sweet and bread eaten in secret is pleasant, but do not forget that all those who did these before you are found dead and are now guest in hell.

- Wisdom is always on the lips of a child who understands, but the rod is always for the back of him who lacks sense.

- The hands of a diligent child soon gather wealth and riches, but slack hands attract poverty.

- Children, ever wondered why the sun is always said to be so bright; it is because it pays rapt attention in class and does its assignments on time.

- A prudent child makes a glad father, but a foolish one is a constant sorrow source to his parents.

❖ A child who loves to give and share freely grows richer, and he who withholds what he should share suffers want.

❖ A child that desires knowledge must love and embrace discipline, but if you want to remain stupid, hate reproof.

❖ Prudent children ignore insults, and that's why you hardly notice their vexation.

❖ A wise son hears his father's instruction, but a scoffer does not listen to rebuke.

❖ When you sleep or slumber and fold your hands to rest too often, poverty will come upon you like a vagabond and want like an armed man.

❖ Six things the Lord hates, seven is an abomination to him: A haughty eyes, a lying tongue, hands that shed innocent blood, feet that make haste to run to evil, a false witness who breathes out lies, and a man who sows discord among brother.

❖ Hand over your work to the LORD, and your plans will be established.

❖ Little children, it is better to have a little with righteousness than great revenues with injustice.

❖ There is a way that seems right to a man, but its end is the way to death.

❖ The mind of the wise makes his speech judicious and adds persuasiveness to his lips.

❖ Wisdom gives life to him who has it, but folly is the chastisement of fools.

❖ Pleasant words are like a honeycomb, sweetness to the soul, and health to the body.

❖ A soft answer turns away wrath, but a harsh word stirs up anger.

REMEMBER; LAUGHTER IS

MEDICINAL AND

GOOD FOR THE SOUL.

9 798580 460215